The biggest kept secret of the pressing community is that it is a simple process anyone can learn.

ISBN: 9780578479729

Published by

 freddymaze

Comic Book Pressing and Cleaning

A how-to guide

2019 Edition

Jacob Gadbois

j.gadbois

To my lovely wife and children, who put up with my craziness and mental unavailability during the last push to get this project out the door, and to my parents, for teaching and proving that anyone can master any skill at any time of life.

Foreword

Pressing and cleaning is not considered restoration by any professional grading companies as of this date of writing. That is not likely to change, as when done properly it is undetectable and many of them have pressing and cleaning services in-house as well.

Pressers keep their craft very secret, and there is much misinformation and speculation as to how we do it. Sometimes it seems magical, what can be done to improve a grade. I am going to give out these secrets, make them public.

Amateur pressers are damaging comic books without the proper knowledge, and misinformation is running rampant across the community. These secrets need to be told, and I aim to do so.

These days, grade is so important. The difference in value from one grade to the next can be astronomical, especially in high grades.

If done properly, a good press and clean can add thousands, sometimes easily tens of thousands in value to a comic book. On some extremely rare and popular books it could be the difference in hundreds of thousands of dollars. Pressing is becoming a big business, and contrary to what those folks will say, it is not this magical skill that only a select few in the world can learn. Anyone can learn it in this book.

There is a popular term "C.P.R."(crack, press, resubmit). This refers to the act of finding a book in a particular grade that through the process of cleaning and pressing can realize a much better grade, and as such, a hefty profit. It is an extremely enjoyable experience to start with a 2.0 book, CPR it, sell it, buy the next grade up with the money, and keep it going until you have a very high grade book with very little invested. In the span of just a few years, one can take a book valued at 1,000, and CPR flip it into a book valued well over 20k.

Please note that I will not be using this book for promotion of my services, and will not press your comics for you. I press for myself, and for close friends only these days; pushing the envelope, experimenting with new techniques, and just generally having fun. Doing it professionally seems to ruin the enjoyment for me, and I find it so much more fun as a hobby. Updates to this book each year will come from my own experience, and from the user community feedback.

I hope that you enjoy this new hobby (or profession for some of you) as much as I do!

BEFORE

1940 Superman #6 in 4.0 Grade 2019 Estimated FMV ~$1,600.00

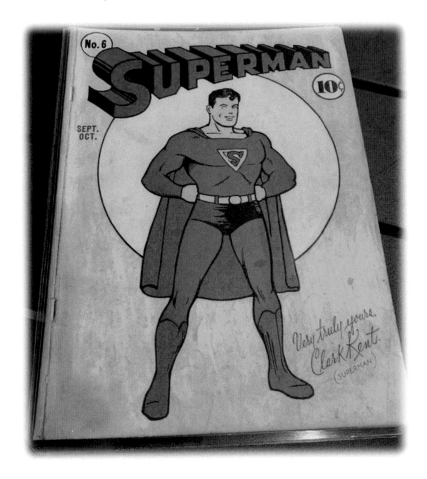

AFTER

1940 Superman #6, 2019 Estimated graded FMV ~$3,000.00

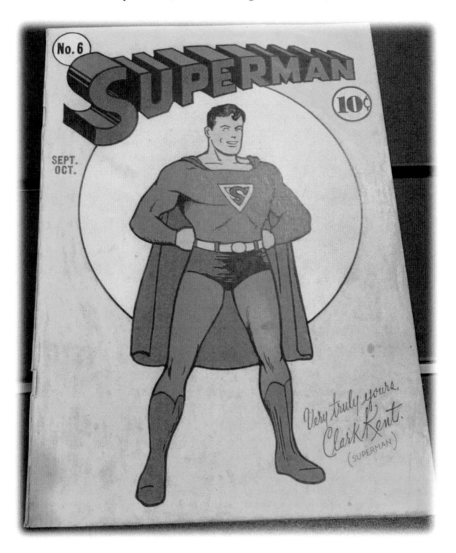

Dry cleaned and pressed.

BEFORE

1939 Four Color #nn (#1) 2019 Estimated FMV ~$1,000.00

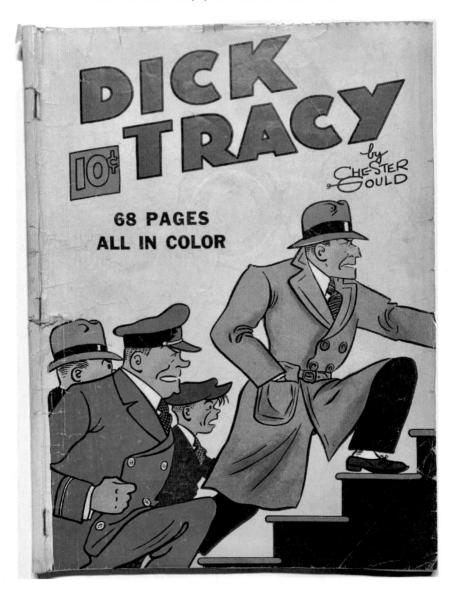

AFTER

Dry Cleaned and Pressed, Estimated FMV ~$3,500.00

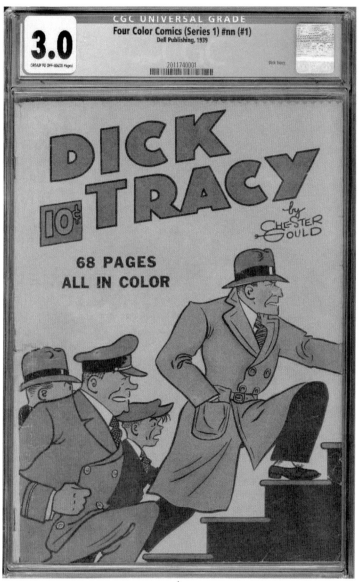

The CGC company does not endorse any techniques described in this book, nor is afilliated in any way with the author , publisher, or methods described herein.

j.gadbois

Should you be aware of any techniques believed to be better, please reach out to us at ComicPressing@outlook.com with the subject line "Feedback". Your ideas/suggestions will be tested, and if they are used in the next book, you will be given credit by name reference. Please note that any and all content received and used will be used without royalty.

j.gadbois

THIRD PARTY NOTICE

The author and publisher of this book presents the information as a Do-It-Yourself (DIY) project and all DIY projects are purely "at your own risk". As with any DIY project, unfamiliarity with the tools and process can be dangerous. Information herein should be construed as theoretical advice only.

If you are at all uncomfortable or inexperienced working on these projects, please reconsider doing the job yourself. It is very possible on any DIY project to damage your book, create a hazardous condition, or harm or even kill yourself or others. The author and publisher will not be held responsible for any injury or loss due to the misuse or misunderstanding of any DIY project herein. You should therefore consult a trained professional of your choosing, and the same is true of other disciplines where expertise is gained through education, experience, and skill-building.

By using the information contained herein, you agree to indemnify the publisher Freddymaze publishing ("Publisher"), Jacob Gadbois ("The Author"), their officers, directors, employees, agents, distributors, affiliates, subsidiaries and their related companies for any and all claims, damages, losses and causes of action arising out of your breach or alleged breach of this agreement.

The materials herein are distributed "as is" and appear in this book without express or implied warranties of any kind, except those required by the relevant legislation. In particular the Author and Publisher make no warranty as to the accuracy, quality, completeness or applicability of the information provided.

The materials provided in this book are for entertainment and promotional purposes only. You may not rely on any information and opinions expressed in it for any other purpose. Neither the Publisher, Author, nor their officers, directors, employees, agents, distributors, affiliates, subsidiaries and their related companies are responsible or liable for any loss damage (including, but not limited to, actual, consequential, or punitive), liability, claim, or any other injury or cause related to or resulting from any information contained herein.

Company names, products, logos, trademarks and any other proprietary intellectual property or otherwise belongs to the rightful owner, which is not the Author nor the Publisher. You should not assume, even if a company name is in this book, that there is an express, implied, or otherwise agreement, joint venture, partnership, or other relationship between us as website proprietors and any of these companies that are discussed merely for educational or other purposes.

Nothing offered by the Author and Publisher should be considered personalized investment advice. While the Author may describe techniques that can increase the value of items, he cannot help you with specific investment questions and decisions, as he nor the Publisher are licensed under securities laws to deal with your particular investment situation. No communication by him should be construed as personal, individualized investment advice. Investors should not rely on the information given by him to make investment decisions.

When in doubt, consult the hired help of your choosing, as you are ultimately responsible for your own use of the information herein.

CONTENTS

There are infinite ways to complete a task; results are what matter most.

1
GETTING STARTED

It is advisable to read this entire book, including the troubleshooting section, before attempting to perform any of these techniques.

Introduction to Pressing and Cleaning

Comic books have made a huge comeback in recent years, and more and more people are using professional grading companies. "Pressing and cleaning" comics has emerged as a non-invasive way to bring a book back to life without restoration, giving the owner an easy grade bump. In the comic community, restoration is generally defined as adding something foreign to a book with the intent of raising the grade. Pressing and cleaning does not add anything to the book, and thus is not considered restoration.

While developing a pressing and cleaning technique, keep this in mind; it is not restoring books. The goal is to repair or remove what defects are possible without adding anything to the book.

The purpose of this book is to guide in the right direction, learning how to press and clean books without damaging them, and getting good results. To be clear, if you try these techniques, you will damage your first books as during practice; so be sure to start out with ones that are worthless.

The term "Pressing" is almost always used to describe this entire process. It is likely that the folks who simply throw books into a press and call themselves "Pressers" just don't know any better and have taken the term literally. Pressing is so much more than just, well, pressing.

What Pressing and Cleaning Will Fix

Bends

Folds

Dents

Creases

Spine stress

Most stains

Sun/Dust shadows

Tanning

Impacted corners

Rippling

Spine rolls

Pencil writing

Most Foxing

Dirt

Fingerprints

Foreign substances

What Pressing and Cleaning Will Not Fix

Color breaks

Missing pieces

Most ink writing

Tears of any kind

Fading

Sometimes a trade-off must be decided upon. This coffee stain is mostly gone, but the paper is degraded, and some other defects exacerbated (notice the white defect areas). Was it worth it?

Saving Thousands With Better Results

It can cost thousands of dollars for this simple service. Those pressing fees add up quickly, and professional pressers tend to refuse old and brittle books as well. Knowing how to do it will make things easy, and better results than the pros can be achieved when the right amount of time is put into a book.

Professional pressers cannot make a good living by spending the required time on some books. Once learned in the process, you will understand this much better. Certain books require hours of time, whereas a pro may spend a few minutes and move on, telling you that the defect just wouldn't come out, or, more often than not the honest ones will simply refuse to work on it. You can be in control over this process; only you should decide how much time should be spent on any particular defect. If you are looking to become a pro, this is also a good place to start!

In the following chapters, it will be assumed that the reader possesses a certain amount of common sense. Instruction such as using a flat surface to work, a clean surface, washing one's hands, etc., will not be reminded.

Skip to the Fast-Press

Most modern (all glossy) books just need a quick wipe-down with a cotton round or Absorene pad, a few pieces of buffer, and right into the press. This is a very quick process and one does not have to perform all the techniques described in this book to get 9.8 results. Once you have a good understanding of each chapter, consider what a good fast-pressing method will be for certain books.

As an example, one fast press method for modern all-gloss books would be:

- Wipe down book with cotton round
- Place non-glossy backing board at centerfold
- Place non-glossy cardstock between front cover and interior pages
- Silicone release paper around entire book
- 5 sheets non glossy paper to top and bottom of book to complete the buffer
- Place book in press, heat to 160 and switch off press.
- Once press is cold, remove the book and buffer materials.
- Grasp the spine lengthwise and fan through the pages to ensure nothing is stuck together.

Simple enough for a fast method, but will not get great results on soiled, stained, spine rolled books. This fast method will take out small spine stresses, finger bends and light soiling, and is used by many to get quick 9.8 grades on modern speculation books.

Cooking With Books.

Cooking is a good analogy, as each of us will, over time, develop our own recipes. Pressing and cleaning are multi-stage tasks, and each book with each unique defect requires a tweak to your recipe. All paper from all eras is not created equal. Golden age paper is so much different than modern age paper, and a completely different recipe is required when working on the two different books.

Some folks use the "smash" recipe. These are those that go out and buy a press, and simply heat and squish books in it. Sure, that will take out just about any bend or fold in the paper; but the book comes out with a razor-sharp spine, structurally damaged, and obviously pressed. There is so much more to a recipe than simply putting a book in a press and turning it on. Don't be the guy making crepe's out of comics when the pros are making nice fluffy pancakes.

Remember, a good press and clean is undetectable when properly finished.

The Pressing Process

This section will serve you as a general guide overview; a "forest-view" look at the process for you to refer to.

With few exceptions, these processes must be done in order. As an example, do not start with pressing, then cleaning. The last thing you want to do is heat press all the dirt deep into the paper fibers. We may not need to do all of these, but this is the general order of operation, if the section is applicable to the book.

1. Hand tooling
2. Cleaning
3. Humidify
4. Wash
5. Tacking iron
6. Build a buffer

7. Heat pressing
8. Cold pressing

Some books will only need #s 2-6-7, and some will need the entire process. Identifying each scenario will help you move through piles of books at a much faster rate.

Detecting Restoration

A good presser should be able to identify all defects in a book, which includes restoration. Color touch, glue at tears in the pages, and tape are common. These can all be fixed and/or removed in the process, which is covered at the end of Chapter 3.

Color Touch and Tear Seals

The most obvious way to look for color touch is bleed-through. Inside the front cover at the spine, one can see the marker that was used bleeding through to the other side.

Look for places in the paper where the color should be broken and white, but is not. Places on the cover where it is rough, yet the color is still present. Very bright LED light is great for this. UV lights will not detect all forms of restoration, but can be helpful. Never rely entirely on a UV light to detect restoration (in fact, some of the top professional graders do not use one at all).

Lift the cover and shine a bright light through the paper, looking at it from the other side. You may notice areas here that stand out. Almost all color touch and tear seals will show up in this transparency test.

"Feel" the book. Running a finger over suspect areas can confirm color touch, glue, paper seals, etc. The texture will be noticeably different in some cases.

Married Pages or Cover

A married page will almost never be the same exact color and size as those around it, staples will have been manipulated to accomplish this, and will never line up exactly. Out of all the wraps married, centerfolds are most often the culprits. Unfortunately, a married page cannot be fixed.

- Look for manipulated staples, new staple holes, uncharacteristically widened staple holes.

- Check the color and patina of the page against those around it, along with the edge of the paper under magnification. The edge of the page is most often a quick tell, as most books have not been subject to the same type of dirt/grime over time.

- The size of the page matters. On older books, no

two books are exactly alike due to older cutting processes that had loose tolerances. Two pages being close to the same size is not as much of a tell, but sometimes they are noticeably different.

Trimming

Trimming is widely considered the worst of all restoration, and will decimate the value of any book. It is not technically "restoration", but is deception in its greatest form. To detect trimming, one must understand how a book is put together. Take 20 sheets of paper and fold them in half like a comic book. Notice how the edge opposite the spine is in a "V" shape? The thickness of the folded spine shows up on the opposite edge, and most often this is cut off straight if the book has been trimmed.

- Look for the V shape of pages on the right side

- If the book was opened and laid out flat and trimmed at an angle one side at a time, the V shape will be present. However, each page will be slightly angled in its cut. The edge of each page should be a square cut, not angled.

- Look at the edge of the pages for color differences. If the right side of the book is a brighter color than the top and bottom, it has been trimmed.

- The outer fibers of a page will always be darker

than the inner fibers on older books, especially those with slight interior tanning. Look for an edge where the paper color is brighter than its own page.

Thinner silver age books, especially with a slight spine roll, can be extremely difficult to spot trimming as there is no discernable "V" shape to spot. This book has plenty of weather on the edge, no square cut pages (the page edges look "fluffy" from age), and the color is all correct.

Pressing Materials Needed

- <u>Heat Press</u>. You'll need a decent press that has uniform pressure and controllable temperature. Seal, D&K, are good brands, but expensive (although they can be found used). Cheaper "t-shirt" presses can be found on Amazon, but one must ensure the pressure and temperature is adjustable, and the plate may need to be polished. Minimum size should be that of a folded flat comic book (about 11x15). Personally, I own several of both styles and actually prefer the cheaper swing away arm (that is not convenient) but the circle of springs for even plate pressure and ease of the pressure adjustment knob is great.

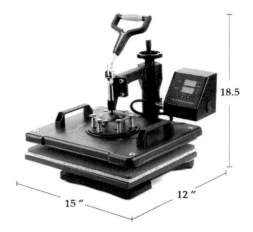

18.5

15 "

12 "

- ¾ (.75) Polished Hardwood 15"X12", or ¼ (.25) Inch X15"x12" Flat Steel Plate. Use this at the bottom of the press sometimes rather than the silicone pad to eliminate the need to flip books in the press.

- A Box of Old "Kids Comics". Golden age to modern age books. Trashed junk books usually found in the kids section can be found at your local comic store for very little money. These are great for practicing on!

- Magnifying Glass. Purchase a high quality one you can look through comfortably for long periods without getting dizzy.

- Gloves. I don't recommend them unless working with peroxide, as it desensitizes your grip, and damage can be done to fragile books. Washing hands every half hour or as needed is best.

- <u>Silicone Release Paper (SRP)</u>. Often used for baking and backing for stickers, there are many choices out there. Get something that is not textured!

- <u>Small Manipulating Tools.</u> A home dental kit, and small screwdriver kits.

- <u>Eraser Set</u>. From very soft, to kneaded, to very hard. We want a good variety here. #2 pencil erasers as well, as the grip on the pencil helps. Erasers that "crumble" during use are best, as they do not hold dirt and are less abrasive, thus less prone to pulling off color.

- <u>Round Balls</u>. Either ball bearings, or white smooth hard plastic. Must not be textured.

- <u>Zero Gloss Comic Book Backing Boards, Various Sizes.</u> Do not ever use off-brand ones that have any kind of gloss (it could melt into a comic!).

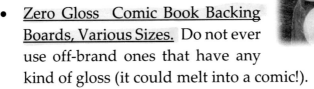

- <u>Bright LED Work Light.</u>

- <u>Distilled Water.</u>

- <u>High Quality Paint Brush.</u> This is used for brushing shavings away and keeping the workspace clear of debris

- <u>Tacking Iron</u>. Any small iron with temperature control will do here, but a mini iron with various attachments is preferred.

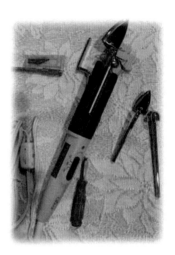

- <u>Multipurpose Paper.</u> The type used in a home printer. You will burn through this at a very high rate; suggest getting a box of reams. No gloss!

- <u>Cardstock Paper, Varying Weights (no gloss).</u> This is for use under the cover of the book. Too thin and indentations will not come out in a fastpress, too thick and the paper will cause its own crease in the cover of a book in the press.

- <u>Small Smooth Needle-nosed Pliers (No Teeth).</u> For manipulating staples.

- <u>Plastic Paint Scraper, Various Sizes.</u>

- <u>Cotton Rounds.</u> Smooth, no texture, can be found in cosmetics aisle.

- <u>Absorene Pad.</u> Your greatest weapon against dirt, pencil, and fingerprints on glossy books.

- <u>Wet Wipes.</u> Unscented, ⚠ no soap (water only).

- <u>Humidity Chamber</u>. There are two types of chambers; store purchased and custom D.I.Y. While the do-it-yourself chamber is effective, it carries risk and cannot provide precise humidification like a beverage cooler. Further detail is provided in Chapter 5, Humidification. Recommended purchase is a beverage cooler with clear glass door, refrigerant control shut-off, and flat shelves (Danby model DBC026A1BSSDB or similar).

2

HAND TOOLING

Never perform hand tooling on defects that require paper manipulation without first
humidifying, you may break the piece off or break color!

Pressing Books by Hand

To start, remove any defects that can be done by hand. These include complete folds, small bends, hanging pieces, loose staples, and any other item that can easily be manipulated. Unfortunately, one can expect to run into plenty of boogers as well.

Inspect the Book

Find any and all defects. Identify which ones need humidity before hand tooling. It is helpful to use a very bright LED light here, and UV helps to see some odd defects such as certain staining and misc. gunk.

Heavy Small Indents

Someone may have at one point written a letter on top of a book. This leaves heavy indents on the book underneath the letter, and these can be removed. Writing directly on a book sometimes leaves these indents as well. You may even see a seal that looks like something a notary would stamp with.

Clean off any debris that is over this area (Chapter 3). Place a backing board under the area in question. Use a ball and carefully roll it over the indentation(s). The ball will smooth it out. If the indentations are especially heavy, you may need to use a tacking iron. This is a small iron set on low heat. Place a sheet of SRP paper over the area, and heat with the tacking iron. Once heated, the paper is much more pliable, but keep in mind that means it is weaker as well. Remove the paper and continue rolling until the defect is completely gone. There will likely be rippling around the area that has been rolled, but that will easily flatten once the book goes to heat pressing. The important thing here is to just get those small indents out.

Another method for stubborn indents or folds, one can use a heated ball to roll it out. Note the use of SRP paper between the ball and the cover. This tool is detailed in the Chapter 1 materials section, and further instruction on the various uses is at the end of this chapter.

Some small writing on covers denotes an important pedigree that is an important part of comic book history. Before removing writing on a cover, one should first research to determine if the markings are more valuable if left alone.

Removing heavy indentations on a Four Color #169 (Woody Woodpecker #1) using the ball rolling technique.

Removing 80-year-old heavy indentations from a Four Color Comics #nn (#1 Dick Tracy) with a heated ball.

Loose Staples

If the staple needs to be cleaned, read Chapter 3 first and do so before tightening them.

Staples should be tight. However, we do not want to manipulate them so much that they break or deform from their original shape. On a normal book, simply open the book to the centerfold, and push the staple ends just enough to tighten them. On a square bound book, the staple ends are located under the back and front cover. Use a small blunt instrument for this, as we do not want to do damage to the surrounding paper! For square bound books, these staples should be extra tight, to prevent them from poking through the cover during the heat pressing process.

Tip: Do not manipulate the staple from the flat (outer) end unless it is bent. This part of the staple should be perfectly straight.

Centerfold Barely Attached

Sometimes this is a fixable defect. Usually it is as simple as opening the book to the centerfold, pushing the paper further into the staple, and tightening. During the printing process, especially on Silver age books, sometimes the staples did not push through the centerfold all the way.

Other times, move the staple prong just a hair to the left

or right so that the staple grabs the paper better. However, this is a delicate process and risky. Ideally this is done after flattening a spine out completely for a re-fold, as the book can be worked on much easier when flat. Refer to Chapter 7 (Heat pressing) for a more detailed process on how to do that. Care must also be taken not to manipulate the staple much, as a conserved grade is possible.

Another option is simply leaving it alone. Place a backing board tight to the paper and staple, holding them where they are until you are done working on the book.

Bent Staples

These can be especially tricky. Tearing the cover while working on a bent staple is a definite possibility. Find a flat (smooth, no teeth) vice grip or pliers that are the same width as a common staple. Position the pliers so that when squeezed, it flattens out the staple. If the staple is tight, first loosen it just a bit, so that you do not grab any paper in this process, as it could tear the cover away from the staple.

Tip: If the book has a bad spine roll, you may have to wait until that is fixed to work on the staple.

Minor Spine Rolls

Minor rolls can be pressed by hand. Open the book to the centerfold, and insert a fullback board or thick backing board, tight to the staples (assuming they are centered, otherwise insert tight to the center. One by one, pull the pages towards the outer edge of the board, effectively repositioning each page perfect to the staples at the edge. If there is a major spine roll, do not attempt this, and refer first to Chapter 7 (Heat pressing).

Another way to fix a minor spine roll is to literally roll it. Use a 1/16 to 1/8" dowel, insert it to the centerfold, and roll it until the spine is where it should be. This is an acquired skill, and has a big risk of damaging the book when done improperly.

Tip: this is one area in which you can jump around the order of operations. Hand pressing a spine roll should immediately precede a bit of heat pressing. You'll want to clean the book before doing this technique so that you can put the book right into the press to ensure the paper stays where you put it. Don't forget to build your buffer before heat pressing (Ch 6).

Stickers and Tape

Stickers and tape can usually be picked right off after a few hours in the freezer. Alternatively, with a hair dryer or heat gun. Do not overcook the sticker, as it may burn it into the pages. Once removed, if there is any residue leftover, it can usually be removed by tacking some painters masking tape onto the surface and pulling it off. Do not use anything but painters' tape; we do not want to pull off color.

⚠
Light Moisture

The following defects that can be hand-tooled require moisture before performing. Using a cotton swab that has just a small drop of distilled water on it is preferred. Use only just enough to get the job done. If you use too much water, "tide lines" will appear at the edge of the water spot when it is dried. Although advanced and difficult, these can be removed (detailed in Chapter 4).

Folded Corners

Unfold any corners that are completely folded over, on the cover and inside the book. Do not do this without humidity first if the bend or fold is sharp (it may break off!). Take a damp cotton swab and lightly touch it to the bent/folded area to wet the defect first. This will ensure the bend or fold is pliable.

Tiny Folds/Tears

Use small tools here with a magnifying glass, and remove any tiny folded over paper or small tears on the field portion of the cover. Be careful not to damage any surrounding paper. Do not do this without humidity first if the bend or fold is sharp (it may break off!) Take a damp cotton swab and lightly touch it to the bent/folded area to lightly wet the defect first. This will ensure the bend or fold is pliable, and if on the cover with print, will lessen the chance of a color break as well once it is moved. Ensure that the paper is not visibly wet, as this could cause a water "tide line" to appear.

Hanging Pieces

These are especially tricky. Move them back into place especially carefully without tearing them further, using the same technique described for folds. These are usually located at the edges of the book. Bindery tears at the top and bottom of the book should be moved back into place as well.

Misc. Gunk

Dried boogers, pieces of food, or other foreign matter can often be cleaned off easily with a dull plastic paint scraper. If one does not humidify first here, the foreign matter may take pieces of the book with it when scraping it off. These should be loose before removing. Take a damp cotton swab and lightly touch it to the foreign matter to wet the defect first. This will ensure it is not effectively "stuck" to the book before removing it. Another method is to use a no-soap wet wipe. Be careful not to push or smudge the gunk into the book; wipe and pull up, don't push down.

Tacking Iron

The tacking iron falls under "hand tooling", but must be done AFTER Chapter 3, Dry Cleaning and Chapter 5, Humidification. A tacking iron can be any iron at all (full size clothes iron, tacking iron, mini iron), and is used to remove defects with heat before the book is ready for a heat press. Smaller irons are preferred, especially those with controllable heat settings.

One must get a "feel" for the iron in use, but NEVER heat it over 180F. Even at that temperature the book can get color bleed, and normal use should be 150-160F.

Heavy bends, folds, creases, spine bends, finger bends, and other specific defects can be removed with this tool. Working out the small defects with a Tacking Iron is ideal before heat press, unless fastpressing a book that has small easy defects (See Chapter 7, Heat Pressing and Chapter 1 for details on the fast press method).

Some square bound books have wrinkles on the binding glue. A tacking iron can take these out easily, while putting the book into the press without doing so will simply fold these small wrinkles into tight lines that will never come out.

Tips on Use of the Tacking Iron

- 150-160F regular temperature, bumping to 180F for quick trouble spots only on older books.
- Ensure that the iron is completely clean before use.
- Use a backing board or cardstock paper behind the page being worked on. If the paper gets ink transfer on it, you are using too much heat.
- Dampen the defect before working on it, with either a humidity chamber, a very small spray of steam, or a damp cotton swab
- Know that after use, the page will be wrinkly and distorted around where it was ironed. This is normal, and the page will flatten entirely in the heat press.

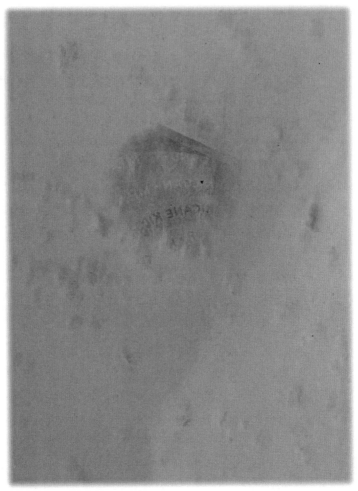

This backing board was used under the cover while applying a heated ball and tacking iron. The indentations are normal, but the color transfer is not. This is an example of applying too much heat while using a tacking iron and/or heated ball.

3

DRY CLEANING

Never heat press before cleaning, and never clean a book until the humidity level is returned to normal (applicable if you have humidified the book prior to hand tooling).

Dry Cleaning

Any book can be dry cleaned, just know that there are different methods for different aged and different paper quality books. You should have a range of tools at your disposal here, from very soft gum erasers, to hard vinyl erasers. See the shopping section in Chapter 1 for more detail. This step should be performed before using a tacking iron, washing, or heat pressing.

Staples

"Conservation" can devalue a book significantly. Staple cleaning falls under this category, unless it is done carefully and not too invasively. If the staple has a small bit of rust or grime, this can be easily cleaned. Think more in terms of "polish".

Use a hard eraser on the outer surface and simply clean it, being extra careful not to touch the paper! Use a magnifying glass here, as one can easily rub off paper color.

If the staple is tight and you really want it very clean, there is the option of loosening it. Go to the centerfold and very carefully loosen the prongs just a touch while holding the outside flat area with pliers so as the staple does not rotate. Less is more here, do not manipulate staples any more than absolutely necessary; getting them back in place perfectly is difficult and this process carries a very high risk of damaging the book. This method takes much practice and should be avoided until one is extremely confident in their ability.

Foil and/or Heavy High Gloss Books

These are the books to be most careful cleaning. Foil scratches easily, and an eraser will often leave streaks. It is best to stick with non-abrasive materials such as sponges, wet wipes, Absorene pads, and cotton rounds.

An Absorene pad cleans off just about any dirt, pencil, and grime easily on high gloss books. Always start with this tool on these types of books.

Golden Age Books

Start off by lightly wiping the entire book cover with a cotton round and/or Absorene pad. This will remove the loose debris. Surface oils such as fingerprints can usually be removed in this process as well.

Use a regular #2 pencil eraser or another soft/crumbly eraser and lightly go over the entire book. Don't spend much time on any specific area to start. At the edges, be careful not to pull any corners or tears apart further. When moving the eraser, make sure to place two fingers on either side of it to stabilize the paper, especially at the edges of a page. Leave the shavings in place so that you know where you've been until the entire side of the cover is done. Brush away the excess with a fine paint brush. Do the same to the spine and the reverse cover. Do not push harder than the weight of the pencil itself.

The white areas can now be cleaned a bit harder, as there is no color to worry about, but there is still gloss there on most books so one must be careful not to strip that as well.

Once done, move on to the more specific bad sections. Sometimes, a defect penetrates the gloss of the book. At this juncture, you must decide which is worse; no gloss, keep the defect, or wash the spot (Chapter 4). In the case you decide that no gloss is better, move to heavier erasers, being careful with a magnifying glass to be sure you are not stripping too much gloss nor stripping off color. Make sure the eraser has sharp corners to work these areas!

Bear in mind that some grime is just embedded too deeply in these older books, and getting it out is just not worth stripping off the color or gloss of the book. Sometimes a no-soap wet wipe will do the trick, but do not bear down hard and one must be careful not to let it "wet" the book while wiping. If that does not work, refer to the more advanced technique in Chapter 4, Washing.

Finish up the cleaning with a ball of Absorene. Roll it out over the cover lightly, but do not push hard as it can penetrate the paper fibers and stain your book pink. This material is good for pulling out additional dirt and polishing the cover.

Looking under bright light at an angle, you may notice a bit of "streaking" from your eraser. This can be polished off easily with some fine linen or a cotton round.

Clean your erasers on a scrap piece of paper often!

Use only the weight of the pencil, do not push. Erasers that "crumble" are best as they are less abrasive.

Silver Age Books

Use the same process as previously discussed under Golden Age books, keeping in mind that there is a bit more gloss on these and heavier erasers can strip off gloss or leave streaks much easier. Sponges and cotton rounds work well.

Wet wipes can be used, but again, use sparingly and be careful not to let it "wet" the book. Be sure to wipe off any excess a wet wipe may leave behind immediately– you do not want it to penetrate the paper fibers.

Bronze Age to Modern books

Absorene pads are the best tool for cleaning books with higher gloss. Erasers can still be used in the Bronze and Copper Ages, but more sparingly. The glossier the book, the more effective the Absorene pad and cotton round tools.

Once wiped with the Absorene pad, use an eraser on the white areas, being careful to avoid color, as it is stripped off easily. Crumbly erasers work best as they are not as abrasive. When moving the eraser, make sure to place two fingers on either side of it to stabilize the paper, especially at the edges of a page. A straight ruler or drawing template is best used as a guide.

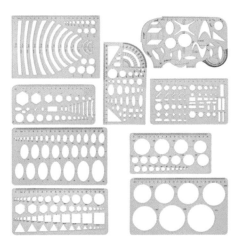

Finish up your cleaning by wiping/polishing the book with a clean cotton round.

Wet wipes can be used here, but again, use sparingly and be careful not to let it "wet" the book. Be sure to wipe off any excess a wet wipe may leave behind immediately– we do not want it to penetrate the book.

Universal cleaning tip: do not worry about creating rippling on the cover while cleaning; this will all come out easily in the heat press.

Amateur Restoration and Conservation Removal

Here we will cover the very basics of amateur restoration removal. Professional restoration removal should be done by a professional restoration expert, as their methods and means are very different than ours, and they are capable of removing their style of work easily. Most restoration can be removed, and sometimes one must decide the lesser of two evils. As an example, an amateur may have touched up a color breaking spine tic with a sharpie. That kind of restoration is almost impossible to remove, unless one decides to literally remove paper. On an expensive book, it may be worth doing if the value is there.

Tape Removal

Tape can usually be removed with a hair dryer or heat gun. Do not overcook the tape, as it may burn into the pages. Once removed, if there is any residue leftover, it can usually be removed by tacking some painters masking tape onto the surface and pulling it off (only on newer glossy books). Do not use anything but painters' tape; other materials may pull off color. Another method to use is to place the book in the freezer, and once cold, pull the tape off by hand.

For more difficult tape, it is possible to remove it and most of the brown stained residue with a touch of pure Naphtha. Be especially careful purchasing this material, as some brands have additives that will stain the book. This method is very effective, but takes testing and a practiced hand.

Color Touch

Amateur color touch is usually easily removed with a utility knife razor, or X-Acto-type knife blade, by scraping with the edge. Do not saw at it. Note that you will uncover an area of the book that has no color, and it will not be pretty. Be careful to stick to the color touched area; we do not want to remove any color that is original! Professional color touch can be removed with much less invasive methods, and should be left to those professionals.

Tear Seals

Tear seals can be very hard to detect, but if done properly are usually water soluble and can be removed easily. If an amateur used superglue or something similar, sometimes the only way to remove it is by literally cutting it out. If it is water soluble, refer to the next chapter of this book (washing) and apply those techniques.

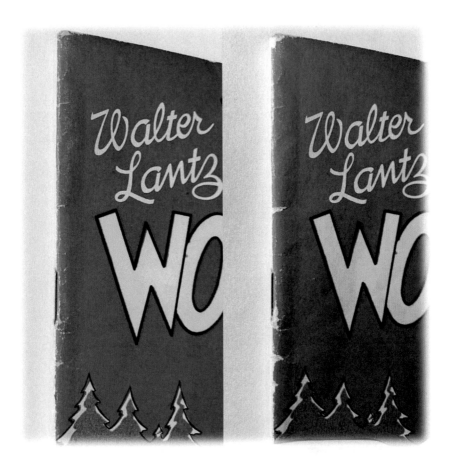

Amateur color touch under bright LED lighting can visibly be seen on the left where the paper should be white. Colors do not simply fade in lines on a book, they break and become white. On the right, a sharp utility razor replacement blade was used to remove it, exposing the true white paper.

4

WASHING

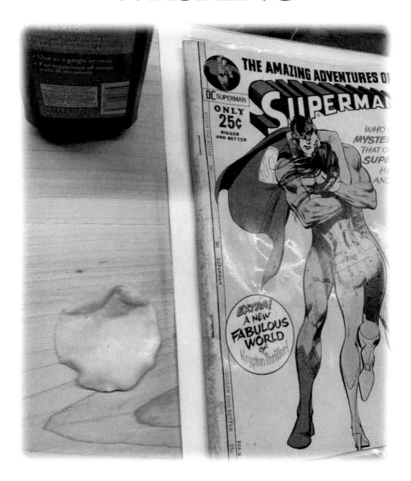

This area of the book is mostly, but not universally accepted by comic book collectors, and some still consider this restoration (some still consider general dry cleaning to be restoration as well). Use and publicly talk about this technique at your own risk.

⚠
Done improperly, this technique can and will deteriorate a book.
⚠
Performing this technique over signatures is not recommended.
⚠
Newer age modern books (all glossy interiors) do not take well to washing, and one will likely damage the book.

The Basics of Washing Without "Restoration"

Chemical washing is a detectable restoration, and will devalue a book significantly. Filtered and distilled water, and even H2O2 (Hydrogen Peroxide, standard 3% solution bottle) is a great alternative as it naturally breaks down into oxygen and water in ultraviolet light (drops the second oxygen leaving only H2O, which then evaporates), and in my experience leaves no residue when done correctly. Because there is no residue, this technique is viewed my most as not restoration, as nothing is being permanently added to the book, but rather things are being removed. This may come as a surprise to some, but there are many books in "blue labels" that have been washed.

Many professional pressers are using steam to remove tough defects, and the use of water is widely accepted in the community. When using only water, this chapter simply takes that material for a different use.

This technique will remove stain tide lines, lift dirt, remove foxing, remove or significantly lighten dust and sun shadows, and brighten white colors.

Before and after of a successful peroxide wash treatment of heavy foxing, and spine roll pressing.

Order of Operations
Inspect
Protect
Apply Solution
Pressure
Repeat
Rinse

Inspect the Book and Choose a Method

If a book has a various mixture of grime and foxing, coating the entire cover is likely best. If it has just a few trouble spots, doing a partial coat will work well. It is recommended to practice many times on various defects before attempting on anything of value. If normal dry cleaning will suffice, there is no need to wash.

Water or 3% Hydrogen Peroxide?

Water is the best choice for things such as general filth and tide line stains, and is much less invasive on the paper fibers. Water will only lift foreign matter from the paper, whereas Peroxide will both lift and lighten. Soda stains, foxing, and heavily embedded grime will need a Peroxide treatment for removal. Never treat a book with Peroxide if it does not need it.

⚠

If using a peroxide solution, make sure to wear gloves.

Protecting the Book

Start by protecting the inside pages. If you will be washing the spine along with the cover, you must go to greater lengths.

If you are only doing spot treatment or just one side of the cover, simply slip a large magazine bag in between the cover and pages, and as you work be careful to ensure it remains in there tight.

To protect the spine for a wash, cut strips of poly bag, and slip them through between the staples, pulling through the other side, then placing a full bag in between the cover and inside pages. In this scenario, the only unprotected part of the inside pages will be around the staples, so take care around these parts and be mindful of that.

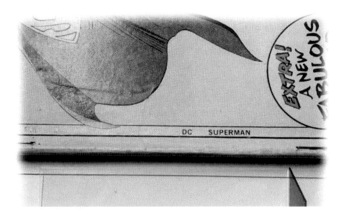

Cutting a polybag to slip through between the staples

Three sections of polybag wrapped around the book entirely underneath the front cover to the back, to help protect the side of the wrap under the cover, after which a full bag is placed between the cover and interior pages.

Applying the Distilled Water or Peroxide

First protect the book as detailed previously. Place two pieces of blotter paper underneath the book. Dip a smooth cotton round in the solution (distilled water, or Peroxide). Very lightly wet the entire surface of the book and the spine. Remove any excess by placing a paper towel onto the cover and removing it immediately. If using peroxide, *do not rub* at this point, it could remove color. If using water, light pressure is OK, but take care not to apply pressure once the paper is wet. Pick up the book by one of the sheets of blotter and carefully flip the book onto the bottom sheet of blotter, then do the back cover if needed. Do not fully saturate the paper if possible.

If the stain penetrates both sides of the page, more solution is needed. If not, only lightly coat one side of the page so that it does not saturate through as there is risk of creating tide lines on the opposite side.

Foxing or bad staining is very easily seen at this juncture, as they will darken very much. Do not worry about this darkening, as it will dry much lighter than it was. It is recommended to take a picture of your work while these areas are wet and darkened so that you may easily identify the areas if spot treatment is needed.

Low Heat or Cold Press

Insert acid free buffered blotter paper on either side of any washed pages. Alkaline buffer is helpful in removing any existing acidity in the book, which will help mitigate any natural off-gassing in the future, but is considered by many to be "conservation". It is not very important here, and not worth the risk of a conserved grade.

If the blotter on top of or below the book immediately becomes saturated, replace it. Place a heavy piece of MDF or something similar that is flat and heavy on top of the book if cold pressing, or insert the package into the press at low heat (120F, switch off on entry). The reasoning for this pressure is so that any off-color staining on the paper is absorbed into the blotter rather than back into the page.

⚠

Once wet, be extremely careful handling the book, as the cover will tear away from the staple very easily!

Once the book has dried (about 20 minutes or so for cold pressing, or once the press has cooled), re-coat if necessary, or move onto spot treatment for trouble areas.

⚠

If using a peroxide solution, each coating is deteriorating your paper fibers. Be mindful not to apply too many coats.

If you choose to coat only the front or back cover, be careful not to create tide lines where you stopped applying the treatment. This can be done by feathering in moisture, detailed in the next section for spot treatment.

Spot Removing Foxing, Stains, and Tide Lines

First protect the book as detailed previously. Use a fine tip cotton swab for this technique. Carefully (without rubbing) dab the trouble areas liberally with the solution to wet them. You will notice a water line; this must be "feathered" into the surrounding areas, or you will create your own tide lines that will need to then be fixed.

Very conservatively wet a cotton swab with solution. Use this to go around the edges of the very wet areas. Do this until you do not see any strong wet lines under a magnifying glass. If the exact wet line can be seen, you may create a tide line when the solution dries. Remember, never rub wet paper; only dab. The abrasive rubbing can easily strip off color.

Do this as many times as you like for trouble areas. Cola and coffee stains are the most troublesome, and they may take several days of coating and re-coating to make them disappear, although it may not be worth it, as each coat degrades the paper.

Remember to place blotter paper on either side of the area in which you are wetting, and place something dense on top to press them together for moisture absorption.

Tip: Your book will be wrinkly after it dries. Do not worry, this will flatten out perfectly during the heat pressing process in Chapter 7.

Spot treating a coffee stain with H2O2 (Peroxide).

Stain tide lines after just a single water treatment and press.

Rinsing

It is strongly recommended to rinse the book after any Peroxide wash, to restore PH and remove any residual solution. This is done the exact same way as applying solution, except you will now use filtered distilled water at all areas that were treated.

There is no need to rinse if only H2O (water) was used.

j.gadbois

5

HUMIDIFICATION

Be extremely careful handling a humidified book, as the paper is malleable and more fragile than normal in this state. Never attempt to rub pages or use anything abrasive as the risk of paper damage is too great.

Introduction to Humidification

Humidifying a book is important to do for several reasons, and it is rare that a book will not require it. Reversion, which is when the book literally reverts to its prior state to pressing, is a very high risk when humidity is not used. Paper is basically made with water and various wood fibers; introducing humidity helps loosen them to re-align these fibers to where you want them; heat and press alone is not completely effective in doing this as the fibers will only bend, rather than shift. Not humidifying a book also raises the chances that a non-color breaking defect may break color during heat pressing.

Humidifying a book should be done immediately preceding the use of a tacking iron, buffer and heat pressing, and all hand tooling and cleaning should be complete at this juncture.

Building a Humidity Chamber

There are two popular ways to build a chamber, and although effective, the DIY version is not recommended; it is cheap, however. The concept is to use water in a sealed area to raise humidity around a book. It is recommended to have a humidity meter inside the chamber so that one can monitor the levels as well.

Out-of-the-box Chamber

A "beverage cooler" with a clear glass door is the best chamber (see shopping list, Chapter 1). Ideally, it has a control to shut off refrigeration, and a controllable internal light so that you may see inside. If you cannot find one with separate controls, either forego the convenience of the interior light, or internally disable the refrigeration. This makes a great sealed unit. Never operate the chamber with refrigeration, as cold will tighten paper fibers; you are simply buying it for the good insulated seal and internal lighting.

Place a humidity monitor inside, and purchase additional racks if needed.

Purchase a container that will hold water, that fits nicely at the bottom of the unit. Fill this with filtered distilled water. A large bowl with good amount of water surface area is recommended, as the more surface area of water there is, the faster it will evaporate into the air of the chamber.

Most options come with wire racks. Use a backing board under a book when putting a comic on the rack, or install your own smooth shelves.

Temperature and humidity meter on the inside of a chamber. Note the temperature in the chamber should be very close to the temperature of your workshop to mitigate the chance of condensation.

DIY Chamber

Clear storage tubs with a good cover that seals well can be used to create a cheap but effective chamber.

⚠

A storage tub is not a good insulator, and therefore can and will create condensation inside, especially if the temperature outside the tub is different than the workshop. You must be very careful of this, as water dropping onto a book can create tide line staining.

The bottom of the tub is essentially the water container; pour the distilled water directly to the bottom. Alternatively, for a bit more control, use a water container.

Purchase several 3-or-4-inch Schedule 40 PVC couplings. These can be found in the plumbing aisle at most hardware stores (they are for joining two pieces of pipe). Place them face up in the bottom of your container.

Cut a square shelf to fit inside your container with plenty of space on the sides, and place it on top of the couplings. There is now a shelf suspended above water.

Example of a DIY humidity chamber storage tub

Using a Humidity Chamber

Place a small bucket or bowl of water inside, and close the chamber door.

Once the chamber reaches 90% RH on the monitor,

remove the container of water and place your book inside. By opening the door, the RH likely lowered, so be sure that the monitor is reading at least 75% after placing the book inside. With a DIY chamber, you may not have the option of opening it and must simply leave the water and book in there together, as the opening is so large the air may exchange too quickly.

It takes about 4-6 hours for the average comic to acclimate to the RH set. Once done, the book is now ready to move onto working with heat, tacking iron, and/or pressing. The book can be left in a well-insulated chamber 24 hours without fear of damage, although it is not recommended on books with signatures.

Every chamber is different, and it is recommended that you practice with yours to get a good "feel" for how long it takes. The book should not feel very damp; it is simply humid.

Cleaning the Chamber

Mold spores flourish in a humidity chamber. When it is not in use, leave the chamber open, unsealed. When using the chamber often, clean it with bleach spray once per week, making sure to let it dry out 100% before using it again. The last thing you want to do is have a moldy chamber!

⚠

Extra care must be taken for signed books. Humidity can cause signatures to run or become blotchy. Use as little as possible, if at all when working on signed books. Sharpie and paint pens can easily bleed.

j.gadbois

6

BUILDING A BUFFER

Never put a book into a heat press without proper buffering, and never use any kind of buffer materials that have added gloss.

Preparing a Book for Heat Press

"Buffering" is an extremely important step in this process, and one must never put a book into a heat press without doing this. Done improperly, one can create razor sharp spines that break color, squish square spines, and stick together pages just to name a few pitfalls.

Many pressers' solution to those issues is simply low pressure in the press or extremely low heat. When a book is buffered properly, one can apply plenty of pressure without worry. We will review this process for both square bound (also known as Prestige) books and normal spines (also known as Saddle Stitch).

What we are essentially doing here is adding enough various materials to the interior of a book to ensure the spine is not flattened nor stretched to break, or adding more to un-flatten it, along with protecting the pages from each other and the heat of the press.

Centerfold Buffer

Start with the center of the book. Take a non-glossy backing board that is just a hair thicker than the staples (gloss usually melts at 170F, do not use gloss!), and place it next to the spine. Mark the location of the staples. Carve out a quarter inch of material. We are making room for the staples at the centerfold. Insert the board at the centerfold, tight to the inside of the paper. The staples should no longer be in the way. Look at the edge of the book to ensure that the board can be inserted all the way. There should be no gap between it and the inside paper at the spine.

Golden Age Through Modern (Non-glossy Interior) Front and Back Cover Buffer

On most comics aside from newer moderns, the cover stock is of glossy paper and the inside is cheaper paper of varying types. For these comics, the cover can possibly stick to the inside pages, or bleed ink onto them. Insert a cut to size sheet of SRP (silicone release paper) between the cover and interior pages, front and back.

Add a piece of 65-110lb cardstock paper (smooth) between the SRP and interior pages. This will give the interior a bit of hardness for pressing out defects in the cover.

Cut a piece of large SRP and fold in half. Insert the entire book. Alternatively, simply put a piece on top and bottom of the book.

Add 3-5 pages of paper to the bottom and top of the previous SRP. This is used to absorb any imperfections in the pressing plates, and mitigate the possibility of pressing loose debris from the press into the book.

Worded Example of Golden Age Through Early Modern Age (Interior Pages are Not all Gloss) Saddle Stitched Books with the Actual Comic Book in Bold

3-5 pieces paper

SRP

Cover of comic

SRP

65-110lb cardstock

Interior pages

Carved board or pad at centerfold

Interior pages

65-110lb cardstock

SRP

Back cover of comic

SRP

3-5 pieces paper

⚠

Lower the lb rating on the cardstock if the book is extra thin; we do not want to "stretch" the spine when pressing, so take care to look at the edge of the built buffer to ensure there is enough room.

Modern Books (All Gloss Pages) Front and Back Cover Buffer

Modern books are buffered the same way, but do not need the interior SRP, as the pages are completely glossy throughout the book and must be pressed on lower heat.

Worded Example of a Modern Book's Buffer with the Actual Comic Book in Bold

5 pieces paper

SRP

Cover of comic

65-110lb cardstock

Interior pages

Carved board or pad at centerfold

Interior pages

65-110lb cardstock

Back cover of comic

SRP

5 pieces paper

Tip: Additional buffering may be used as needed to add "air" to the finished product, however, keep in mind that too much buffering can stretch a spine and break it.

Square Bound (Prestige)

Can you press a square bound book without crushing the spine? Of course. In fact, one can even un-crush a square bound spine with proper buffer, in a press with pressure!

Inspect

Carefully inspect the edge of the book. Is the spine crushed? Is the spine thicker than the rest of the book? If the spine is crushed, follow the "**Un-crushing a spine**" section below. If the spine is thicker than the book, follow to "**Basic Buffering**".

Basic Buffering

Older square bound books are stapled through top to bottom, rather than from the side. Ensure that you have lifted the cover and tightened these staples to the point where they are not poking out (we don't want to poke them through the cover during pressing).

There is no need to buffer the center of these comics, as there are no staples there.

Do NOT add cardstock between the cover and interior pages here, as the book will end up with a line at the interior edge, as one cannot insert the cardstock all the way to the inside of the spine (the existing cover glue will stop it).

Insert a cut to size sheet of SRP (silicone release paper) between the cover and interior pages, front and back.

Buffer the interior to match the spine thickness, using non-glossy multipurpose paper. Insert the pages as far inside the book they will go. Do not add all these pieces to one single place, scatter them evenly throughout the interior pages. Use a straight-edge and check the edge often while adding pieces, until the entire book is as thick as the spine, looking at it on edge. Once buffered, it is now impossible to crush the spine.

Cut a piece of large SRP and fold in half. Insert the entire book. Alternatively, simply put a piece on top and bottom of the book.

Add 3-5 pages of paper to the bottom and top of the previous SRP.

Tip: Simply building a spacer in the press next to the spine will not suffice, as pressure is needed to remove any cover defects.

Worded Example of a **Square Bound** Book's Buffer with the Actual Comic Book in Bold

5 pieces paper

SRP

Cover of comic

SRP

Interior pages

Buffer (as needed for height to match spine)

Interior pages

Buffer (as needed for height to match spine)

Interior pages

Buffer (as needed for height to match spine)

Interior pages

SRP

Back cover of comic

SRP

5 pieces paper

Un-crushing a Spine

Buffering to un-crush a spine is done much the same way as basic square bound buffering. The goal here is to add enough extra interior pages to effectively "stretch" the spine back to its original height.

First, loosen the staples just a touch. The book is almost always thinner than the spine, in this process we will be fattening the book until the spine is fixed – be careful not to rip pages around the staples.

Estimate the prior height of the spine before it was crushed. This may be done with a straight ruler.

Buffer the interior to match the estimated spine thickness, using non-glossy paper. Insert the pages as far inside the book they will go. Do not add all these pieces to one single place, scatter them evenly throughout the interior pages. Use a straight-edge and check the edge often as you are adding pieces, until the entire book is as thick as the estimated prior spine, looking at it on edge. Keep in mind that if adding too much, the spine can possibly rip from stretching it too much in the press.

Once the book is effectively "fattened" out the spine, use the Mini Iron/Tacking Iron and iron the square edge. The heat will loosen the glue and re-set the spine.

Tighten the staples with a blunt instrument, very tight so that they do not poke through the cover in the press.

Cut a piece of large SRP and fold in half. Insert the entire book. Alternatively, simply put a piece on top and bottom of the book.

Add 5 pages of paper to the bottom and top of the previous SRP.

Worded Example of a Crushed Square Bound Book's Buffer with the Actual Comic Book in Bold

5 pieces paper

SRP

Cover of comic

SRP

Interior pages

Buffer (as needed for height to match estimated spine)

Interior pages

Buffer (as needed for height to match estimated spine)

Interior pages

Buffer (as needed for height to match estimated spine)

Interior pages

SRP

Back cover of comic

SRP

5 pieces paper

Inserts, Digital Codes, and Other Oddities

These pages must have buffer on either side of them, to ensure there are no imprints made on the adjacent pages during pressing. Standard multipurpose non-glossy paper works well, and enough sheets should be used to absorb the potential lines. Cutting out parts of the buffer paper to accommodate an oddity as well, if it is exceptionally thick.

Tip: backing boards may be used in place of the 5 pieces of paper, but they must be thrown out and can get costly.

Tip: Before re-using ANY buffer materials, inspect them to ensure they are flat and free of both debris or defects.

Tip: Good success has been achieved with using a silicone pad at the centerfold rather than a backing board, as it protects the spine from stretching too much, but it will absorb pressure that you may be counting on for taking out a few tough defects.

j.gadbois

7

HEAT PRESSING

Cold pressing is just as important as heat pressing. Never skip this step at the risk of reversion and various other pitfalls such as flaring of pages.

Introduction to Heat Pressing

At this juncture, the book will have been cleaned, hand tooled, and possibly washed. The book may actually look worse at this juncture, from tacking iron use, wash wrinkles, etc. It is now time to move into fixing spine rolls, removing small various bends, wrinkles, and folds, and the book should be completed at the end of this process.

A heat press will be the greatest tool, yet also the easiest way to ruin the book.

Setting up the Press

Place the piece of hardwood or 1/4inch steel plate (or other hard bottom material that conducts heat) purchased in Chapter 1 onto the bottom of the press, on top of any pads that came with the press. This plate will be the "bottom", and through the book absorb heat and ensure that the book does not need to flip for a double press. The pad below it will act as insurance against too much pressure. Depending on the press, one may need to purchase a thinner pad to accommodate the additional material.

Always set the pressure depending on the thickness of the book. Older 68-page GA books are much thicker, and adjustment is required between those and Modern Age books (thin, all glossy pages). One does not want to put massive amounts of pressure on any book at any point, but if the book is buffered properly, this is much less of a problem. With a press that has visible springs, half-compression on the springs is ideal. Never go past full compression, and if it feels difficult to clamp the press, lower the pressure.

Cold Pressing

This section is out of chronological order of operation, but should be detailed before attempting heat pressing. The act of cold pressing is twofold.

Firstly, a book always must remain in the hot press until the press is cool to the touch, with exception of inspecting the book periodically if needed. Removing it warm can cause fanning of the pages (Flaring) and the book will not lay flat.

Secondly, once a book is complete and cold, if there were many heavy defects, one must account for possible reversion. After heat pressing, while the book is still in its buffered state, place the book in a cold press overnight before moving it to a bag/board. A cold press can be anything heavy and flat. Sheets of 3/4inch MDF (medium density fiberboard) can be cut to 12x12 and stacked for multiple books with a book between each layer (alternate spines front/back so that the stack does not lean). Leaving the book in the press is ideal, but often one has more books to press and that space is at a premium.

Failing to cold press books in any regard can and will cause problems, the worst of which is reversion. Using a fan to cool a book/press quickly will cause excessive flaring of the pages as well. Imagine you have pressed out what you believe to be a great improvement, send it to a professional grading company, only to get it back with a low grade as some of the pressed-out defects returned!

Fastpressing

Use this method when a book has very few, or many easily fixed defects (such as finger bends, light bends, small non color breaking spine tics) and one wishes to bypass any tacking iron work.

A fast press is exactly that. Place the previously buffered book into the press, close the press, turn on the heat to the required setting (see Press settings by Era and type at the end of the chapter), and once ideal temperature is achieved, immediately shut off the press.

After 15 minutes, open the press and inspect the book. The defects should be gone at this point. If so, place the book back into the press and clamp down. If the defects are not gone, start over by reexamining the buffer for possible adjustment, and restart the heat.

Do not remove the book from the press until the press is cold (this could take up to an hour). The book should naturally cool down at the rate the press' steel cools.

After removing the book from the press, hold the spine firmly and fan the pages. You may hear cracking here if any of the ink was melted and re-set; this is not normal, especially on Modern books with all glossy pages. Turn down the heat.

Again, do not use fans or other such methods to quickly cool the press, as cooling a book too fast or removing a hot book can create issues (see Troubleshooting section). Once cool, the book should be done and ready for a bag and board. Most pressers will further cold press from here, but it is less risky not to with a book that had minor defects.

Major Spine Rolls

Any spine roll can be fixed. The method used is to remove the spine entirely, and create a new one!

First, humidify the book in a chamber as previously discussed in Chapter 5.

Find the centerfold, and carefully lay the book flat, on several sheets of 11x17 paper, spine up. NOTE if the book does not have flat staples, use sheets of paper on either side, with a small gap in the middle for the staples to fall into. Do not press staples at an angle as they will tear into pages.

Place the book in the press, with additional sheets of 11x17 paper on top (5 is recommended)

Lower the top of the press very slowly, ensuring the book flattens evenly and no pages are being folded. Use something long and flat such as a flat ruler to help the bottom pages move outward. Do not clamp the press, simply let its own weight down until the book is flattened.

Turn on the press, heat to 150F/65C then shut off the press. Let the book sit for 10 minutes, then remove from the press.

Flip the book spine down, and place a magazine sized backing board to the staples, straight up perpendicular to the flat book. Fold each page up on either side until you come to the cover. The book is now aligned perfectly to the staples.

In cases where the staples are off-center, simply measure to find the center of the book and place the backer board there for the refolding of the spine.

Once complete, leave the magazine board at the centerfold, and place the book into the press with 5 sheets of paper top/bottom with again low heat at 150F/65C and only the pressure of the top plate of the press (no clamp). Heat for another 10 minutes and remove the book.

The book now has a new spine, and is ready to press as normal with proper buffering.

Stubborn Spine Stresses

Sometimes a press will not remove spine stress on the outer edge of the spine, and the tacking iron has failed to do so as well. Refer to the previous section here on major spine rolls to completely flatten the book to work on it and remove these difficult "tics" that way.

Finally, Heat pressing!

Place the previously buffered book into the press, close the press, turn on the heat to the required setting (see Press Settings by Era and type section). Let the book "cook" for 0-15 minutes, depending on the severity of defects that are being pressed out (get a "feel for this on your own through practice). Once complete, shut off the press.

After 15-20 minutes, open the press and inspect the book. The defects should be gone at this point. If so, place the book back into the press and clamp down for the cool-down. If the defects are not gone, start over by reexamining the buffer for possible adjustment, and restart the heat.

Do not remove the book from the press until the press is cold (this could take up to an hour). The book should naturally cool down at the rate the press' steel cools.

Do not use fans or other such methods to quickly cool the press, as cooling a book too fast or removing a hot book can create issues (see Troubleshooting section).

Once cooled, remove the book and place in a cold press overnight before removing the buffer materials and placing in a bag/board.

Press settings by Era and type

- **Golden Age** books have an ideal setting of 170F/76C. Maximum moment-bump to 180F/82C for a fast press.

- **Silver Age** books have an ideal setting of 160F/71C. Maximum moment-bump to 175F/79C for a fast press.

- **Bronze to Copper Age** books have an ideal setting of 160F/71C. Maximum moment-bump to 175F/79C for a fast press.

- **Modern Age Books (Without Glossy Interior Pages)** have an ideal setting of 160F/71C. Maximum moment-bump to 170F/76C for a fast press.

- **Modern Age (All Glossy Pages)** inks are fragile in the press, and the ideal setting is 140F/60C. Maximum moment-bump to 160F/71C for a fast press.

- **Foil Covers** are extremely fragile to scratching and indentation from the interior staples. Proper buffering is extremely important, along with using low pressure. Heat settings are applicable to the era.

- **Heavy Cardstock** covers should be pressed at high pressure with heat applicable to the era.

- **Embossed Covers** should be pressed at very low pressure, with most of the work done with a tacking/mini iron.

- **Signed books**, no matter the era, should never be pressed above 130F/54C, preferably lower.

j.gadbois

8

TROUBLESHOOTING

Nikko Macaspac @nikkotations

Reversion is the single biggest problem for a presser. This is when a book literally "reverts" back to how it was before you started working on it. Not using humidity, no cold press, and simply heat pressing out bends or folds is the most common mistake that leads to these defects coming back later.

DID YOU DO THAT?

Here are some common pitfalls beginners fall into.

Problem	Solution
Buffer paper has ink transfer	Use SRP paper instead of normal paper when under higher heat, or too much heat was used, as you have effectively pulled ink off the comic
Signed book ink bleeding	Do not use humidity on signed books, nor high heat
Book does not lay perfectly flat (Flaring)	After pressing is complete, you must cold press the book overnight

You may have cooled the book too fast after a heat pressing |
| Recessed staples | Lower your pressure, and add more buffer at the centerfold against the staples |

Crushed/Sharp spine	Add more buffer paper and/or boards are needed. Square bound books must have enough buffer for it to be impossible to crush the spine as well
Wrinkling or waviness	Cold press needed while book is still hot
Pebbling (small dents)	Clean your press plates and work area, there may be debris
Stains	Lower your humidity, and ensure to use only distilled water
Pages stuck together	Lower the heat!
Book "crackles" loudly when handled after press	You overcooked it, turn down the heat!
Vertical spine split (split through or just color break)	Too much buffer, you stretched the spine, or no buffer at all was used, and the book is crushed

Staples pushed through cover	Tighten any square bound staples before pressing, and ensure that buffer paper covers any non-centered staples
Staple indents at centerfold	Add buffer paper to centerfold
Cover colors are faded	Turn down the heat
Scratches	Check your work area for abrasive surfaces
Everything looked great a week ago, but now the book has defects!	You did not humidify enough, or cold press long enough. The paper fibers did not re-set and have reverted back to where they were
Water stain "Tide lines"	Too much moisture on one part of the book. If you over moisturize any portion of the book, you must feather it out
Dirt embedded into cover	Why did you press before cleaning?

Broken off piece	Never un-fold a piece of paper without humidifying first, especially on brittle books
Soft eraser is taking off color	Do not push too hard, nor clean a book that has not been returned to normal humidity levels
Cover disconnected from staple	When a book is humidified or washed, the cover can easily tear from the staple. Be especially careful handling the book in this condition.
Color break after pressing a non-color breaking bend/fold/tic	Use moisture/humidity next time. The ink must be malleable before manipulating it
Add your own below	

INDEX

C

D

E

F

I

J

L

M

N

Naphtha · 40

O

order of operations · 24
overcooked · 87

P

page quality · 49
paper · 4, 6, 7, 8, 9, 10, 11, 15, 17, 19, 22, 23, 24, 25, 28, 32, 34, 35, 36, 39, 40, 46, 49, 50, 51, 55, 57, 65, 66, 67, 69, 70, 71, 72, 73, 74, 79, 80, 86, 87, 88
paper fibers · 7, 35, 46, 50, 57, 88
Pebbling · 87
pedigree · 19
pencil · 14, 34, 36
Pencil · 3
pencil eraser · 34
pliers · 15, 23
polish · 32
polishing · 35
press · vii, xv, xvi, 2, 5, 6, 7, 12, 13, 15, 24, 27, 28, 31, 39, 50, 51, 53, 56, 63, 64, 68, 71, 72, 76, 77, 78, 79, 80, 81, 82, 85, 86, 87, 88
pressing · i, vi, vii, xv, xvi, 2, 3, 4, 5, 7, 8, 19, 22, 23, 24, 32, 45, 50, 51, 56, 60, 65, 66, 67, 74, 75, 76, 77, 81, 85, 86, 87, 89
Pressing · iii, vi, vii, xvi, 2, 6, 7, 12, 18, 27, 77
prong · 22
prongs · 32
PVC · 59

R

refrigeration · 57

S

T

U

W

NOTES

NOTES

NOTES

NOTES

NOTES

j.gadbois

Special thanks for your support, hilarity, and friendship to Billy, Chris, John, Matt @ Excelsiorcomix, Mack, Kris, Burt, and the Riggle

j.gadbois

About the Author

For several years Jacob Gadbois has been researching and testing various pressing and cleaning methods. Scouring the internet for information, speaking with professionals, and tuning the craft using the scientific method. His love of the collecting hobby drove him to form the best possible ways to preserve and improve collectible comic books. Jacob is an information sponge and self-taught innovator, previously in life mastering several crafts and skills including Residential Structural Engineering, Carpentry, Electrical work, and Project/Program Management.

Made in the USA
Monee, IL
22 June 2020

34548672R00079